Autumn's here, with hues so bright,
A feast of colors, it's pure delight!
From pumpkin spice to cinnamon rolls,
Let cozy shades fill up your soul.

With maple leaves and woodland walks,
Spiced treats and cider, as nature talks,
This book's your guide to hues so sweet,
For every coloring page you meet.

Mix and match, explore, unwind,
In every color, comfort you'll find.
So grab your pencils, and let's begin,
to brew the autumn coloring magic in!

Embark on an invigorating journey exploring harmonious color combinations inspired by the delights of autumn! The creation of this book was a purely sensory experience − filled with the delightful aroma of baked apples, the comforting yet invigorating scent of pumpkin spice latte, and the freshness of a morning walk in the woodland sunlight.

This book serves as your creative guide, leading you through the captivating realm of colors and their emotional significance. Whether you're an experienced artist or just starting to delve into the pleasures of drawing, painting or coloring, you'll discover a wealth of practical inspiration and within these pages.

Each page of this book focuses on a distinct autumn theme, showcasing a unique color palette and providing insights into the emotions each combination conveys. These palettes are inspired by the sense of comfort derived from the plentiful experiences that are typical of autumn − a season of celebrating the harvest, reaping the rewards of our labor, and preparing for the forthcoming winter months, when we can finally unwind.

I've also included information on complimentary colors to help you create a striking contrast that can make elements stand out, adding vibrancy and visual interest to your artwork.

But that's not all! You'll discover areas where you can apply your dry coloring tools (or insert swatches of wet media) **to compile your personalized collection of coloring materials in a thematic order**. This will enable you to unleash your creativity, allowing your unique style to shine through in your stunning masterpieces.

Last but not least – each palette includes a reference drawing that incorporates all the colors specified in the particular palette. These images, created by AI, aim not to be perfect but to inspire you to step out of your comfort zone and experiment with new color combinations. I trust you will find them as enjoyable as I did in prompting my app to create them.

My goal is to provide you with the tools and inspiration to select color palettes that will bring your artistic visions to life. I believe that color has the power to transform our emotions and a simple drawing into a masterpiece and I hope this book will help you create pieces that you are truly satisfied with whilst enjoying the process. So, grab your favorite art supplies and let's dive into the magical world of colors of autumn delights together!

Yours truthfully,

Joanna Stone

Table of Color Palettes Inspired by Autumn Delights

Pear Tarte Tatin 5
Pumpkin Spice Cake 6
Apple Cinnamon Coffee Cake 7
Pecan Pie Bars 8
Maple Walnut Fudge 9
Spiced Carrot Cake 10
S'mores Cookies 11
Cinnamon Rolls 12
Roasted Chestnuts 13
Cranberry Pistachio Biscotti 14
White Chocolate and Cranberry Cookies . 15
Sticky Toffee Pudding 16
Caramel Apples 17
Hot Apple Cider 18
Ginger Tea 19
Pumpkin Spice Latte 20
Caramel Apple Cider Coffee 21
Butternut Squash Soup 22
Red Curry Coconut Soup 23
Harvest Festivals 24
Rustic Cabins 25
Spooky Stories 26
Maple Leaves 27
Birch Leaves 28
Oak Leaves 29
Gingko Leaves 30
Sweetgum Leaves 31
Autumn Sunset 32
Grapes and Vines 33
Cinnamon-Scented Candles 34
Acorns and Chestnuts 35
Woodland Walks 36

Palette inspired by: # Pear Tarte Tatin

Autumnal Bliss, Warmth, Comfort, Nostalgia, Delight Elegance, Inviting

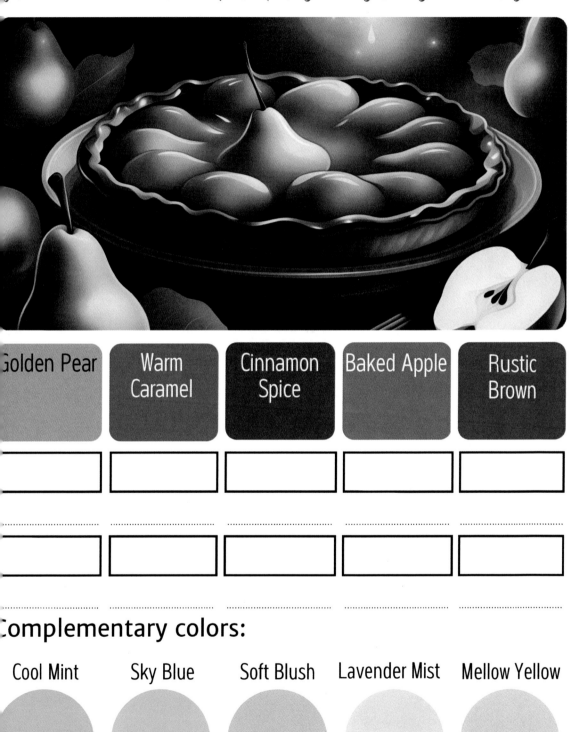

Golden Pear	Warm Caramel	Cinnamon Spice	Baked Apple	Rustic Brown

Complementary colors:

Cool Mint	Sky Blue	Soft Blush	Lavender Mist	Mellow Yellow

Palette inspired by: Pumpkin Spice Cake

Warmth, Comfort, Cozy, Homeliness, Joy, Nostalgia, Contentment

Pumkpin	Cinnamon	Nutmeg	Vanilla	Clove

Complementary colors:

Teal	Navy Blue	Turquoise	Lavender	Forest Green

Palette inspired by: Apple Cinnamon Coffee Cake

Invigorating, Comforting, Sweet, Inviting, Grounded, Rich, Delightful, Aromatic

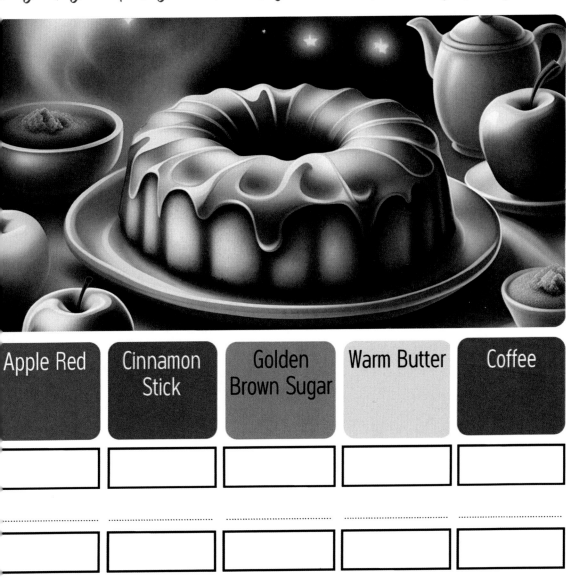

Apple Red	Cinnamon Stick	Golden Brown Sugar	Warm Butter	Coffee

Complementary colors:

Sage Green	Soft Cream	Sky Blue	Lavender	Charcoal Gray

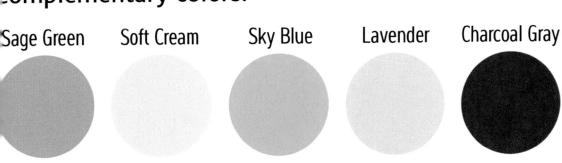

Palette inspired by: Pecan Pie Bars

Warmth, Comfort, Indulgence, Delight, Sweetness, Satisfaction, Hominess

Pecan Brown	Caramel	Harvest Gold	Rich Chocolate	Whipped Cream

Complementary colors:

Cool Teal | Fresh Mint | Deep Blue | Light Coral | Soft Lavender

8

Palette inspired by: Maple Walnut Fudge

Warmth, Comfort, Nostalgia, Coziness, Sweetness, Contentment, Serenity

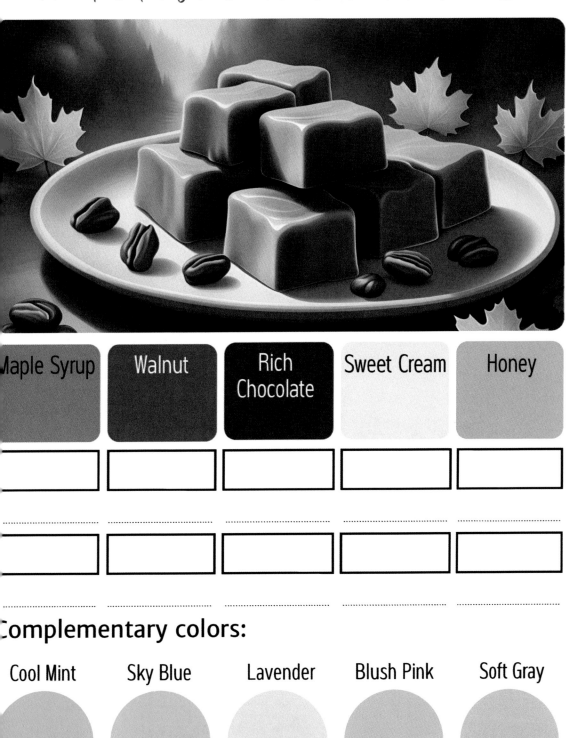

Maple Syrup	Walnut	Rich Chocolate	Sweet Cream	Honey

Complementary colors:

Cool Mint	Sky Blue	Lavender	Blush Pink	Soft Gray

Palette inspired by: Spiced Carrot Cake

Delight, Happiness, Coziness, Joy, Contentment, Invigoration, Sweetness

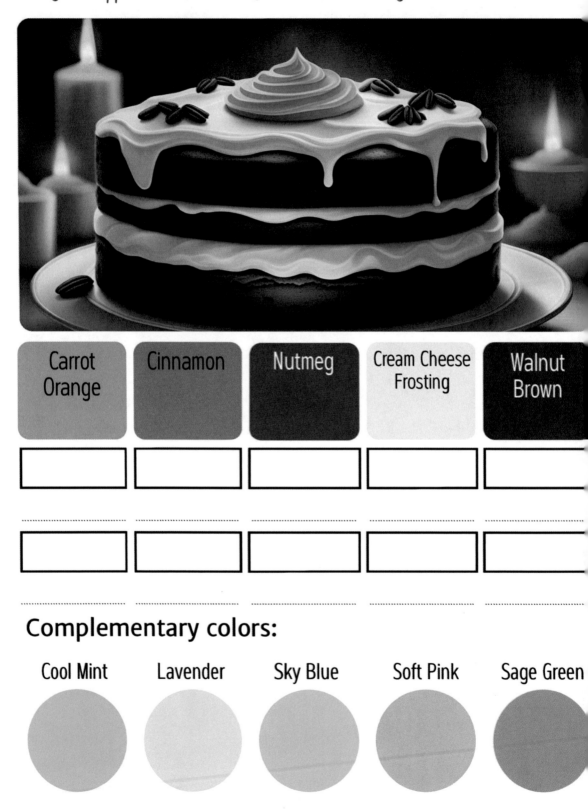

Carrot Orange	Cinnamon	Nutmeg	Cream Cheese Frosting	Walnut Brown

Complementary colors:

Cool Mint	Lavender	Sky Blue	Soft Pink	Sage Green

Joy, Comfort, Delight, Happiness, Indulgence, Sweetness, Togetherness

Marshmallow White	Choocolate	Graham Cracker	Flame	Toasted Marshmallow

Complementary colors:

Ocean Blue	Soft Lavender	Coral Pink	Mint Green	Sunflower Yellow

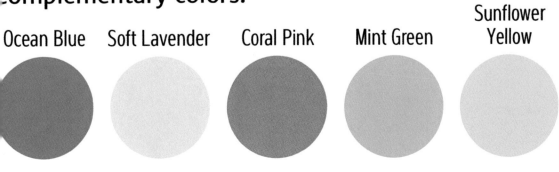

Palette inspired by: Cinnamon Rolls

Comfort, Delight, Nostalgia, Sweetness, Coziness, Satisfaction, Serenity

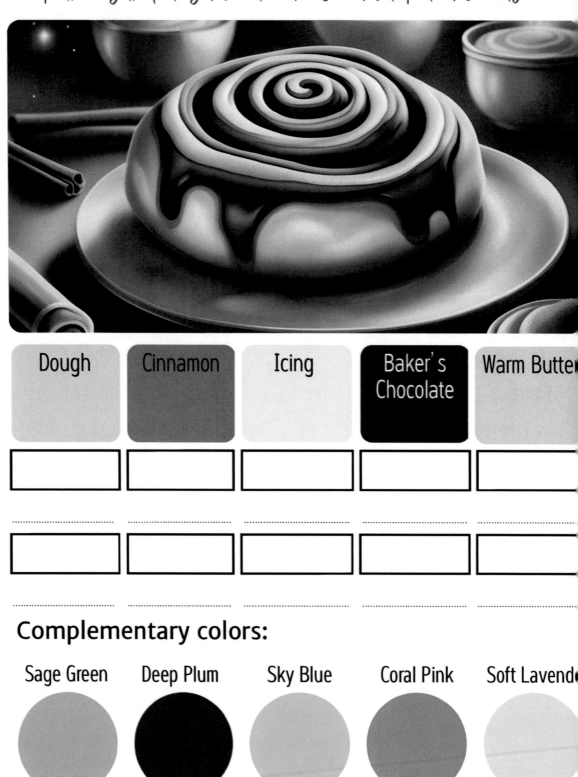

Dough	Cinnamon	Icing	Baker's Chocolate	Warm Butter

Complementary colors:

Sage Green   Deep Plum   Sky Blue   Coral Pink   Soft Lavender

Palette inspired by: Roasted Chestnuts

Comfort, Nostalgia, Homeliness, Serenity, Tranquility, Invigoration, Contentment

Chestnut Brown	Fire Glow	Ash Gray	Toasted Nut	Crisp Autumn Leaf

Complementary colors:

Cool Mint   Ocean Breeze   Soft Lavender   Frosted Berry   Morning Dew

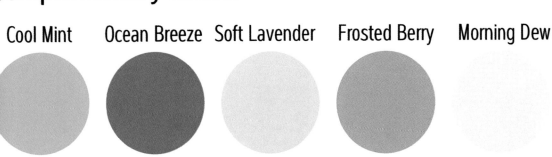

Palette inspired by: Cranberry Pistachio Biscotti

Joy, Sophistication, Cheerfulness, Coziness, Wholesome, Inviting, Luxurious

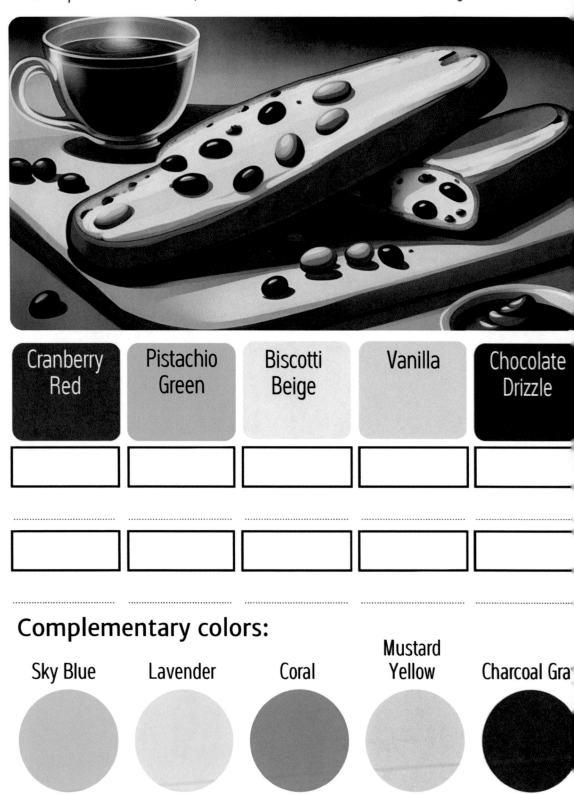

Cranberry Red	Pistachio Green	Biscotti Beige	Vanilla	Chocolate Drizzle

Complementary colors:

Sky Blue Lavender Coral Mustard Yellow Charcoal Gra

Palette inspired by: White Chocolate and Cranberry Cookies

Sweetness, Coziness, Cheerfulness, Indulgence, Happiness, Festivity, Satisfaction

White Chocolate	Cranberry	Cookie Dough	Golden Sugar	Cranberry Jam

Complementary colors:

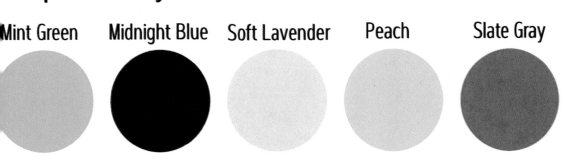

Mint Green	Midnight Blue	Soft Lavender	Peach	Slate Gray

Palette inspired by: Sticky Toffee Pudding

Delight, Sweetness, Satisfaction, Homeliness, Serenity, Luxury, Contentment

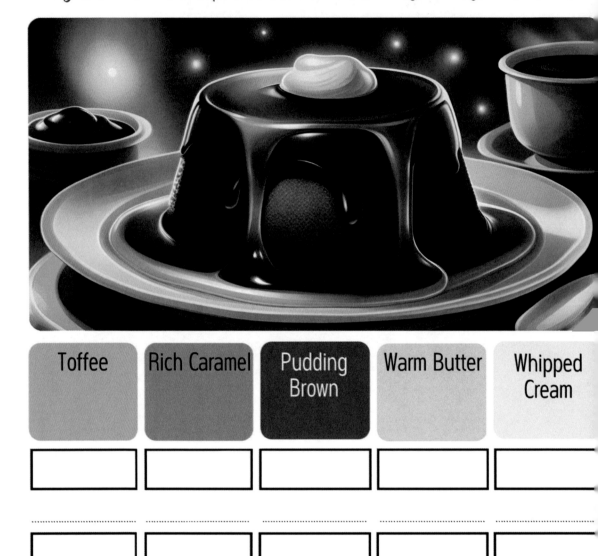

Toffee	Rich Caramel	Pudding Brown	Warm Butter	Whipped Cream

Complementary colors:

Cool Teal	Soft Aqua	Pale Mint	Muted Lavender	Gentle Periwinkle

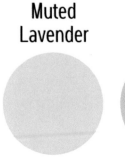

Caramel Apples

Warmth, Comfort, Nostalgia, Delight, Joy, Wholesome, Indulgence, Festive

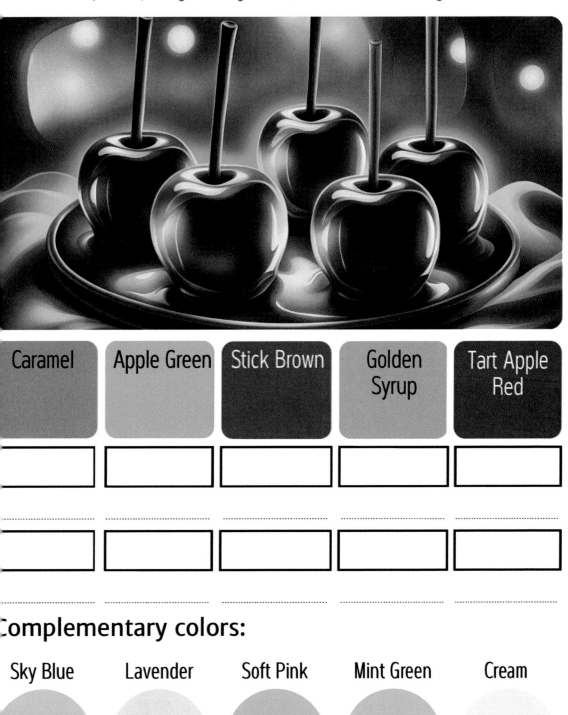

Caramel	Apple Green	Stick Brown	Golden Syrup	Tart Apple Red

Complementary colors:

Sky Blue	Lavender	Soft Pink	Mint Green	Cream

Palette inspired by: Hot Apple Cider

Warmth, Comfort, Nostalgia, Joy, Coziness, Serenity, Delight, Homeliness

Cider Amber	Apple Red	Cinnamon Stick	Golden Honey	Clove Bud

Complementary colors:

Sky Blue	Mint Green	Lavender	Cool Gray	Soft Beige

Palette inspired by: # Ginger Tea

Comfort, Warmth, Serenity, Richness, Stability, Earthiness, Renewal, Harmony

Ginger Root	Autumn Leaf	Warm Honey	Spiced Brown	Tea Leaf Green

Complementary colors:

Cool Aqua	Deep Plum	Soft Coral	Lavender Mist	Mint Green

Palette inspired by: Pumpkin Spice Latte

Comfort, Coziness, Indulgence, Delight, Relaxation, Serenity, Bliss, Contentme

Pumpkin	Cinnamon Stick	Whipped Cream	Nutmeg	Coffee

Complementary colors:

Cool Blue	Soft Lavender	Mint Green	Pale Pink	Light Gray

Palette inspired by: Caramel Apple Cider Coffee

Cozy, Indulgence, Delightful, Bliss, Satisfying, Rich, Autumnal, Heartwarming

Caramel	Apple Red	Coffee Brown	Cinnamon Stick	Golden Honey

Complementary colors:

Sky Blue	Mint Green	Lavender	Cool Gray	Lemon Yellow

Palette inspired by: Butternut Squash Soup

Freshness, Earthiness, Delight, Cozy, Nourishing, Inviting, Homeliness

Squash Orange	Cream	Fresh Herb Green	Nutmeg	Toasted Crouton

Complementary colors:

Coral Pink	Deep Plum	Cool Mint	Soft Lavender	Twilight Blue

Palette inspired by: Red Curry Coconut Soup

Warmth, Comfort, Delight, Nourishment, Harmony, Richness, Vibrancy

Curry Red	Coconut Cream	Fresh Herb Green	Warm Spice	Golden Broth

Complementary colors:

Sandy Beige   Deep Plum   Cool Mint   Soft Lavender   Ocean Blue

Palette inspired by: Harvest Festivals

Gratitude, Abundance, Warmth, Celebration, Joy, Togetherness, Comfort

Pumpkin Orange	Harvest Gold	Maroon	Autumn Leaf	Wheat

Complementary colors:

Cool Teal	Soft Lavender	Midnight Blue	Slate Gray	Frost White

Palette inspired by: Rustic Cabins

erenity, Coziness, Warmth, Comfort, Earthiness, Nature-inspired, Charm

Log Cabin Brown	Warm Fire	Pine Green	Warm Wool	Stone Gray

Complementary colors:

Sky Blue   Sunset Orange   Mint Green   Buttercream   Slate Blue

Palette inspired by: **Spooky Stories**

Mystery, Intrigue, Enlightenment, Timelessness, Calm, Reflection

Midnight Black	Ghost White	Candlelight	Old Paper	Shadowy Gray

Complementary colors:

Twilight Blue	Foggy Mist	Eerie Green	Haunted Purple	Blood Moon

Palette inspired by: Maple Leaves

Warmth, Joy, Enthusiasm, Comfort, Vibrancy, Coziness, Connection

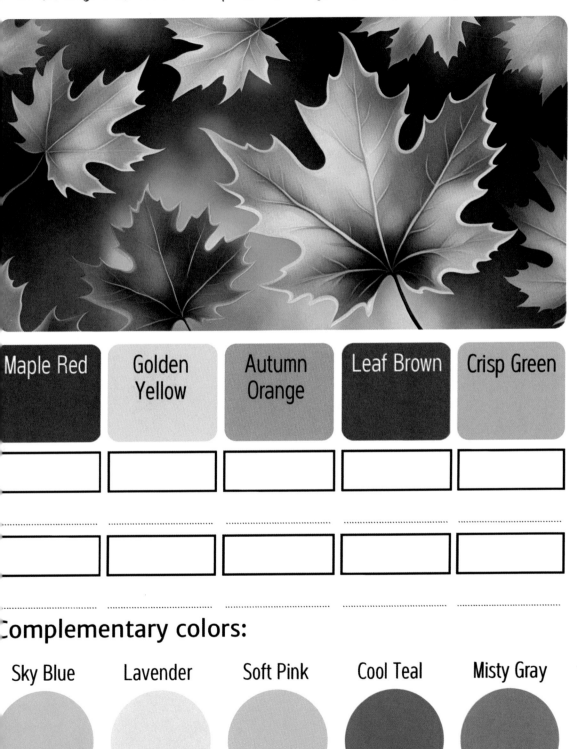

Maple Red	Golden Yellow	Autumn Orange	Leaf Brown	Crisp Green

Complementary colors:

Sky Blue	Lavender	Soft Pink	Cool Teal	Misty Gray

Palette inspired by: Birch Leaves

Groundedness, Stability, Comfort, Calmness, Balance, Reliability, Simplicity

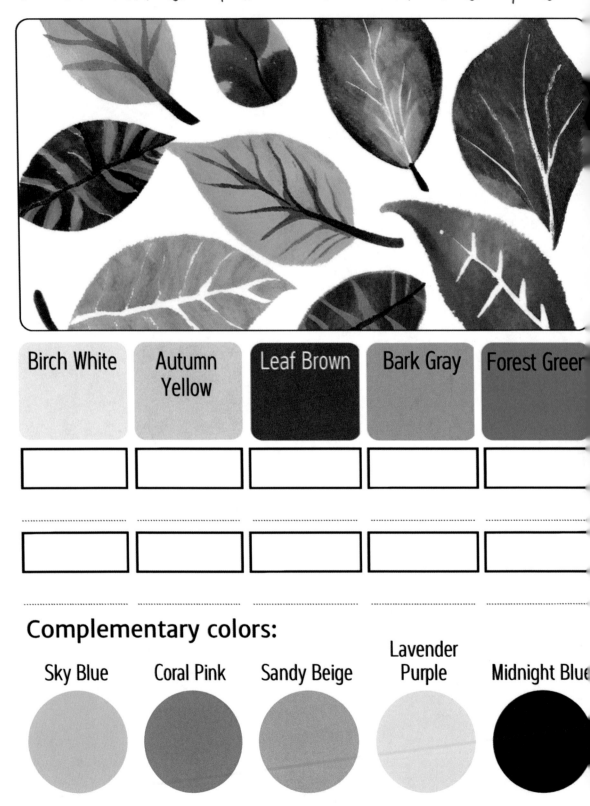

Birch White	Autumn Yellow	Leaf Brown	Bark Gray	Forest Green

Complementary colors:

Sky Blue   Coral Pink   Sandy Beige   Lavender Purple   Midnight Blue

Palette inspired by: Oak Leaves

Warmth, Comfort, Joy, Energy, Passion, Renewal, Harmony, Stability, Vitality

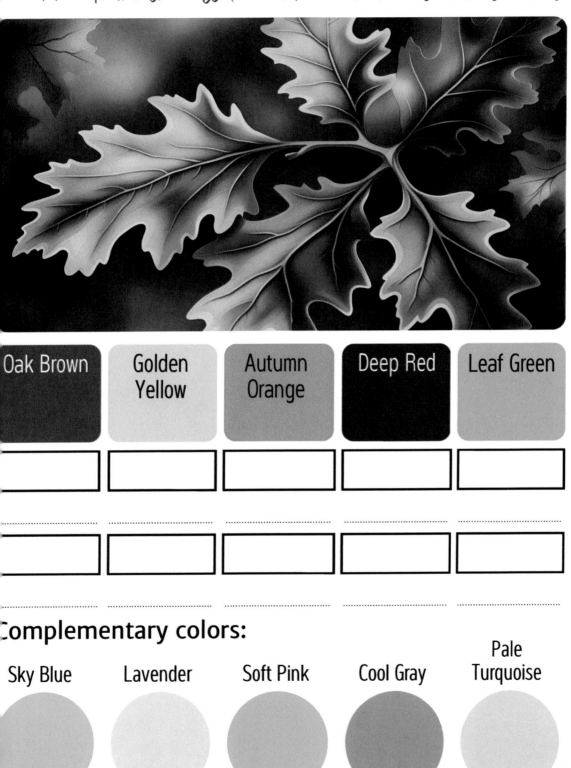

Oak Brown	Golden Yellow	Autumn Orange	Deep Red	Leaf Green

Complementary colors:

Sky Blue	Lavender	Soft Pink	Cool Gray	Pale Turquoise

Palette inspired by: Ginkgo Leaves

Stability, Comfort, Reliability, Earthiness, Security, Happiness, Vibrancy

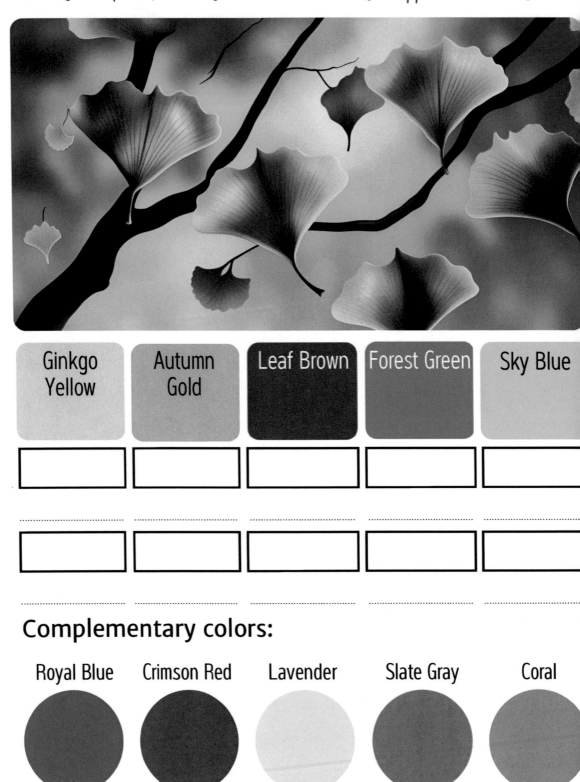

Ginkgo Yellow	Autumn Gold	Leaf Brown	Forest Green	Sky Blue

Complementary colors:

Royal Blue   Crimson Red   Lavender   Slate Gray   Coral

Palette inspired by: Sweetgum Leaves

Passion, Warmth, Vibrancy, Energy, Enthusiasm, Creativity, Comfort, Harvest

Sweetgum Red	Golden Yellow	Autumn Orange	Leaf Brown	Fresh Green

Complementary colors:

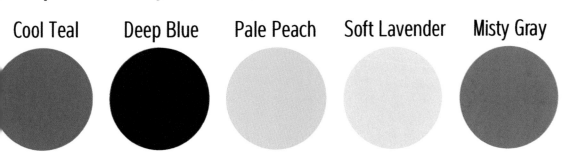

Cool Teal   Deep Blue   Pale Peach   Soft Lavender   Misty Gray

Palette inspired by: Autumn Sunset

Enchantment, Passion, Warmth, Serenity, Elegance

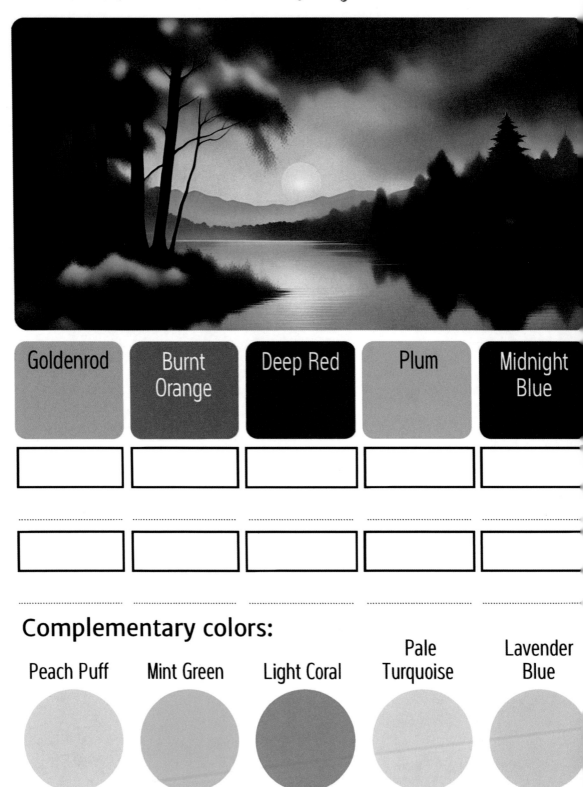

Goldenrod	Burnt Orange	Deep Red	Plum	Midnight Blue

Complementary colors:

Peach Puff   Mint Green   Light Coral   Pale Turquoise   Lavender Blue

Palette inspired by: Grapes and Vines

Serenity, Luxorious, Warmth, Grounded, Renewal, Nostalgic

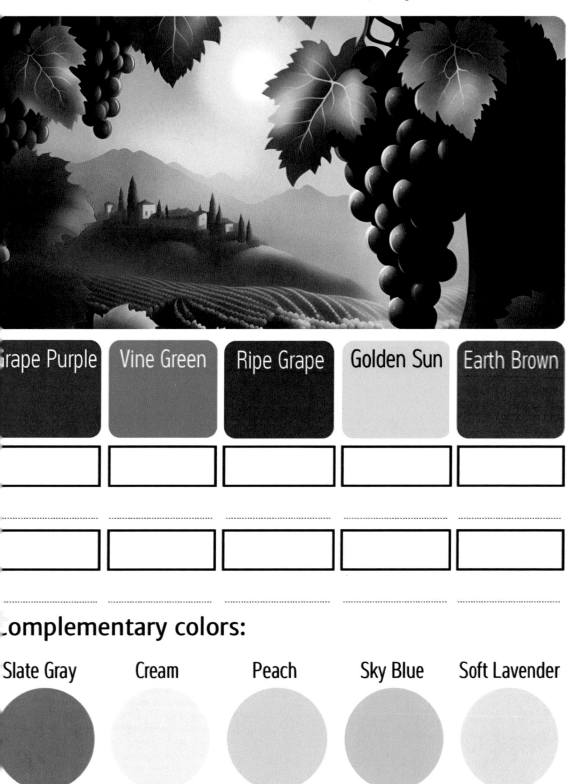

Grape Purple	Vine Green	Ripe Grape	Golden Sun	Earth Brown

Complementary colors:

Slate Gray Cream Peach Sky Blue Soft Lavender

Palette inspired by: Cinnamon-Scented Candles

Ambiance, Cozy, Comfort, Inviting, Warmth, Homely, Serenity, Radiant, Joy

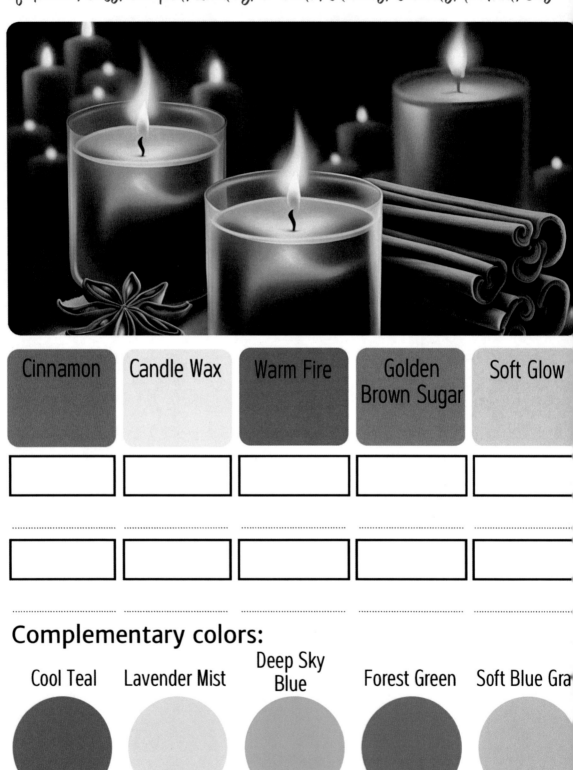

Cinnamon	Candle Wax	Warm Fire	Golden Brown Sugar	Soft Glow

Complementary colors:

Cool Teal   Lavender Mist   Deep Sky Blue   Forest Green   Soft Blue Gra

Palette inspired by: Acorns and Chestnuts

Invigorating, Cozy, Grounded, Elegant, Safe, Natural, Nostalgic, Welcoming

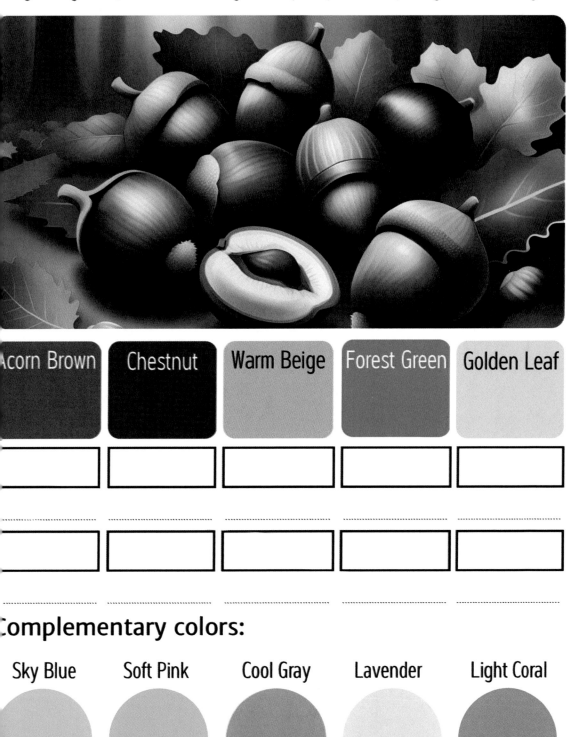

Acorn Brown	Chestnut	Warm Beige	Forest Green	Golden Leaf

Complementary colors:

Sky Blue	Soft Pink	Cool Gray	Lavender	Light Coral

Palette inspired by: Woodland Walks

Tranquility, Warmth, Nostalgia, Grounded, Timeless, Reflection, Stillness

Forest Green	Goldenrod	Chestnut Brown	Maple Red	Mossy Gray

Complementary colors:

Sky Blue	Coral	Lavender	Beige	Soft Pink

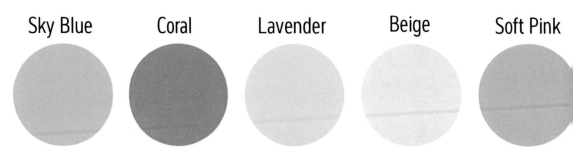

If you've enjoyed this thrilling adventure, make sure to follow my author page on Amazon (amazon.com/author/joannastone) for even more vibrant creations on the horizon! Whether you're experimenting with new color palettes or conjuring up some creative magic, there's always more to explore. Keep an eye out for my Halloween Doodle Book—the perfect companion for testing your spooky and enchanting color combos! Also more thematic color palette books are coming soon to ignite your creativity all year round!

Spice and startlight!

Joanna

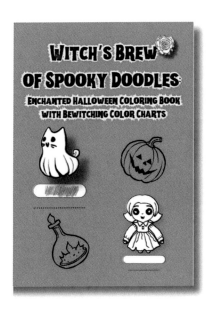

Made in the USA
Las Vegas, NV
08 December 2024

13594360R00024